# SYDNEY

## THE CITY AT A GLAN

### Mrs Macquarie's Point

Gaze out over the harbour fro
the best seats in the city: a ch
into the sandstone peninsula.
*Mrs Macquarie's Road*

### Art Gallery of New South Wales

Come here to see the largest permanent
display of Aboriginal and Torres Strait
Islander art in the country.
*See p044*

### Sydney Tower

Venture to the top of this tower, nicknamed
'Centrepoint' by locals, and on a clear day
you'll glimpse the Blue Mountains (see p102)
to the west and Botany Bay to the south.
*100 Market Street*

### Sydney Opera House

The sails of Jørn Utzon's masterwork were
said to have been inspired by his study of
orange segments. He left the project in 1966,
returning to it in 1999, to design an extension.
*See p010*

### Kirribilli House

The official Sydney residence of the prime
minister was controversially chosen by John
Howard as his main abode.
*Kirribilli Avenue*

### Museum of Contemporary Art

View shows, such as the annual 'Primavera',
showcasing works by young artists, in this art
deco building perched on the waterfront.
*See p078*

### Sydney Harbour Bridge

Sydneysiders simply call it 'the bridge'.
And yes, you can climb to the top.
*See p014*

# INTRODUCTION
## THE CHANGING FACE OF THE URBAN SCENE

'It is beautiful, of course it's beautiful – the harbour; but that isn't all of it, it's only half of it; Sydney's the other half, and it takes both of them together to ring the supremacy bell. God made the harbour, and that's all right, but Satan made Sydney.'

Mark Twain may have written these words in 1897, but more than a century later they couldn't be truer. Sydney is nothing if not a tart – gaudy, proud, gorgeous around the edges but a little sleazy when you scratch below the surface. The Olympic Games in 2000 may have been the biggest party the southern hemisphere has ever seen, but the Sydney balloon still hasn't burst. The city – four million people of 180 nationalities sprawled across an area the size of Greater London – has seen rapid development in the past decade, a lot of it reasonably pedestrian. It's no wonder that a Sydneysider's favourite topic of conversation is real estate – who's buying, who's selling and, most importantly, how much money is involved. For visitors, especially short-term ones, there are five main areas of interest: the city and surrounding harbour, the raffish Kings Cross and Darlinghurst, the bordering neighbourhoods of bohemian Surry Hills and the more urbane Paddington, as well as the increasingly popular Waterloo district.

It is a fascinating place, with the added attraction that you can spend all day, almost every day of the year, in the sunshine. Many come to visit and never leave, which speaks for itself, really.

# ESSENTIAL INFO
## FACTS, FIGURES AND USEFUL ADDRESSES

**TOURIST OFFICE**
Sydney Visitor Centre
*Argyle/Playfair Street*
*T 9240 8788*
*www.sydneyvisitorcentre.com*

**TRANSPORT**
**Car hire**
Avis, *T 9353 9000*
Hertz, *T 9669 2444*
**CityRail**
*T 131 5000*
*www.cityrail.info*
**Taxis**
Silver Service, *T 9020 9966*

**EMERGENCY SERVICES**
**Emergencies**
*T 000*
**Police (non-emergencies)**
*1 Charles Street*
*T 131 444*
**Late-opening pharmacy**
Blake's Pharmacy
*28 Darlinghurst Road*
*T 9358 6712*

**CONSULATES**
**British Consulate**
*1 Macquarie Place*
*T 9247 7521*
*www.britaus.net*
**US Consulate**
*19-29 Martin Place*
*T 9373 9200*
*http://sydney.usconsulate.gov/sydney*

**MONEY**
**American Express**
*341 George Street*
*T 130 013 9060*
*www10.americanexpress.com*

**POSTAL SERVICES**
**Post Office**
*Martin Place, George/Pitt Street*
*T 131 318*
**Shipping**
UPS
*T 131 877*
*www.ups.com*

**BOOKS**
**The Fatal Shore** by Robert Hughes
(Vintage)
**Sydney Opera House: Jørn Utzon**
by Philip Drew (Phaidon Press)
**Oscar and Lucinda** by Peter Carey
(Faber and Faber)
**Rabbit-Proof Fence** by Doris Pilkington
(Miramax Books)

**WEBSITES**
**Art**
*www.artgallery.nsw.gov.au*
*www.mca.com.au*
**Design**
*www.object.com.au*
*www.visualarts.net.au*
**Newspapers**
*www.smh.com.au*
*www.theaustralian.news.com.au*

**COST OF LIVING**
**Taxi from airport
to city centre**
€18.50
**Cappuccino**
€2.50
**Packet of cigarettes**
€7.50
**Daily newspaper**
€0.75
**Bottle of champagne**
€68

**SYDNEY**

**Area**
1,580 sq km
**Population**
4 million
**Currency** A$
A$1 = €0.60 = £0.40 = $0.75
**Telephone codes**
Australia: 61
Sydney: 02
**Time**
GMT +10

AUSTRALIA

□ Sydney
○ Melbourne

Wellington ○

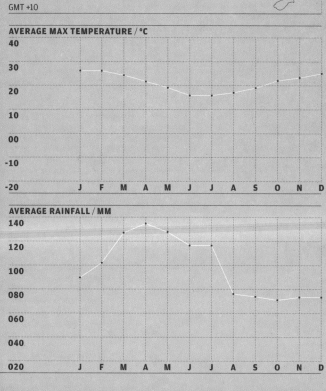

**AVERAGE MAX TEMPERATURE / °C**

| | 40 |
|---|---|
| | 30 |
| | 20 |
| | 10 |
| | 00 |
| | -10 |
| | -20 |

J F M A M J J A S O N D

**AVERAGE RAINFALL / MM**

| | 140 |
|---|---|
| | 120 |
| | 100 |
| | 080 |
| | 060 |
| | 040 |
| | 020 |

J F M A M J J A S O N D

# NEIGHBOURHOODS

## THE AREAS YOU NEED TO KNOW AND WHY

To help you navigate the city, we've chosen the most interesting districts (see the map inside the back cover) and underlined featured venues in colour, according to their location (see below); those venues that are outside these areas are not coloured.

### BONDI

Sydney's world-famous beach isn't nearly as beautiful as some of those to be found to the north of the city, but it is *the* destination for visitors, as well as Sydneysiders, set on a fix of sand, surf and café or bar dwelling; call in at Icebergs Dining Room and Bar (see p062). It is worth noting that the folks who live in Bondi tend to gather exclusively at the north end of the beach.

### SURRY HILLS AND DARLINGHURST

One of the most diverse of Sydney's centrally located neighbourhoods is the bohemian-meets-trendsetting duo of Surry Hills and Darlinghurst. This part of the city has everything – fantastic shopping, eating opportunities and people watching – and it is home to the city's gay community. Much of the area is in the process of being revamped, including the dowdy part of Oxford Street that runs through here, but it is still grungy enough to be interesting.

### WATERLOO

This suburb situated to the south of the city centre is definitely on the rise, and is where retailers who find the high rents of the more established areas suffocating are opening and flourishing. If you have a little time on your hands, walk around the neighbourhood and explore the art-gallery complex and cafés, such as Cafe Sopra (see p058), located on Danks Street.

### KINGS CROSS AND POTTS POINT

There's action aplenty 24 hours a day in the red-light district of Kings Cross, although there are moves by some residents to clean up the neighbourhood. Walk down Darlinghurst Road, which suddenly becomes Macleay Street, and you will find yourself in a much more genteel part of town, Potts Point, where the streets are lined with cafés, stores and glorious 1930s apartment blocks.

### PADDINGTON

The east end of Oxford Street is not only one of the best places to browse upmarket boutiques, but, if you stroll along its back streets, it's a good place to see some excellent independent art galleries and examples of typical Victorian architecture. In the early 1900s, the terraced houses you'll find in the area were considered slum dwellings, but today they are the residences of choice for the city's cashed-up younger generation.

### CENTRAL BUSINESS DISTRICT

The Central Business District (CBD) is not only home to most of Sydney's soaring office towers, but also its most beautiful parks, finest art galleries, restaurants and hotels. Head north and you'll come to Circular Quay on the edge of the harbour, where you can take the ferry to Manly, the Opera House and a revitalised bar and restaurant scene, as well as the historic area known as The Rocks.

# LANDMARKS
## THE SHAPE OF THE CITY SKYLINE

What do people see when they look at Sydney? Locals tend to become somewhat blind to the exquisite natural beauty that surrounds them, although when the sun hits the sails of the Sydney Opera House (see p010) at just the right angle or they spot a grouper (a friendly fish that thinks it's a dog) while snorkelling in Clovelly Bay, they remember how lucky they are. The main landmark, of course, is not even land but water: Sydney Harbour. Entering from the ocean between the North and South Heads, this massive area turns into a number of secret bays and beaches before becoming the Parramatta River.

On dry land, you can get a good overview of the city from the northern side of the harbour – the upper reaches of Taronga Zoo (Bradleys Head Road, T 9969 2777) is a great spot. Just to the east of the CBD is the Horizon (184 Forbes Street). No one is entirely sure what Harry Seidler was thinking when he designed this wavy residential skyscraper, which would look fine in the city skyline but sticks out like a sore thumb in its Darlinghurst position. In the centre of the city is Sydney Tower (100 Market Street), a 305m-tall communication tower that the locals call Centrepoint. If you have a head for heights, go from the street-level shopping centre to the top then take the Skywalk (T 9333 9222). On a clear day you can see the Blue Mountains (see p102). *For all addresses, see Resources.*

### Sydney Opera House

After 14 years of controversy, 'the Big House' opened its doors with a staging of *War and Peace* in 1973. Since then, it has become what some regard as the most important modern building in the world, even though Danish architect Jørn Utzon walked out in 1966 due to budgetary and creative disputes. However, in 1999, Utzon (who has never returned to Australia) agreed to help restore his masterpiece in an A$69m improvement plan. With his son, Jan, and Sydney architect Richard Johnson, he designed a 45m loggia to be added to the west-facing foyers. It was opened in March 2006. In September 2004, the Reception Hall was reopened as the Utzon Room, boasting the venue's first real Utzon-designed interior. *Bennelong Point, T 9250 7111, www.sydneyoperahouse.com*

## Aurora Place

Italian architect Renzo Piano's first Australian project was completed in 2000, and the slender, curved form of Aurora Place stands out as a unique vision among the CBD's forest of uniform office towers. Linked by a glass-covered square that displays artist Kan Yasuda's *Touchstones* sculpture, the building consists of an 18-level residential block and a 41-level office tower, featuring fins and sails in an ethereal tribute to the Opera House (see p010). Elevated plazas that allow people to meet outdoors without leaving the building helped Aurora Place win two of New South Wales' top architecture prizes – the RAIA Wilkinson Award and the Sir John Sulman Award for public and commercial building – in 2004.
*88 Phillip Street, T 8243 4400,*
*www.auroraplace.com.au*

**Bondi Beach**

On a sunny day, as many as 40,000 people can swarm to Australia's most famous stretch of sand. It's not the city's most beautiful beach, but, as with seemingly everything in this town, it's all about location, location, location. Just 8km from the heart of the city, Bondi is a place for people from all over the world, as well as Sydneysiders. They swim, surf, sunbathe and stroll along the promenade that runs the length of the beach. It even boasts its own television programme, *Bondi Rescue*, which premiered in February 2006 and follows the days of the Bondi lifeguards, the all-in-blue professionals who patrol the shore year-round. On the beach itself is another Australian icon, the Bondi Surf Bathers' Life Saving Club (T 9300 9279). Formed in 1907, it's the oldest in the world.

**Sydney Harbour Bridge**
It took almost 20 years for the design of one of Sydney's most iconic structures to be agreed upon, but the world's largest – but not longest – steel arch bridge was finally opened on 19 March 1932. It cost A\$20m to build and was not fully paid off until 1988. By the way, all of its 134m (at its highest point) can be climbed through BridgeClimb (T 8274 7777) – just don't look down.

# HOTELS
## WHERE TO STAY AND WHICH ROOMS TO BOOK

While there is no shortage of accommodation options in Sydney, if you're planning a visit during a peak time of year – say, during the riotous Gay & Lesbian Mardi Gras Festival (www.mardigras. org.au) in March – chances are you'll need to book well in advance if your tastes run more to the boutique end of the market. The city centre is home to most of the big-name chains, such as the Four Seasons at The Rocks (199 George Street, T 9238 0000), Sheraton On The Park (161 Elizabeth Street T 9286 6000) and the newly revamped Hilton (see p030), but the smaller, more fashionable hotels tend to be located in the Darlinghurst district. Our top choices include Mooghotel (opposite) and the colourful Medusa (see p036). For both dedicated business and pleasure travellers alike, Darlinghurst is the perfect base, from where you can walk to the city or the shopping strip of Oxford Street and are surrounded by some of the best bars and restaurants in town.

Quite bizarrely, for a city that prides itself on its beach culture, there are relatively few upmarket hotel rooms with an ocean view. Thankfully, Ravesi's (see p028), which overlooks Bondi Beach (see p013), had a facelift in 2002, and is now the hotel of choice for visiting international musicians and actors. If all the rooms are booked here, take heart in the fact that Bondi is a mere 15-minute taxi ride from Darlinghurst.

*For all addresses and room rates, see Resources.*

## Mooghotel

Things to do before you're 35: discover your inner rock star. Mooghotel is the creation of Simon and Susanah Page, founders of the renowned Australian dance music label Sublime. As you'll be the only guest in the hotel, this has to be Sydney's most exclusive address. There's a recording studio, plunge pool and hi-tech gym, while the white, bright suite has an entertaining area downstairs and an upstairs bedroom with multi-room digital music/video system, bathroom and treatment area complete with enormous free-standing resin bath. A butler, a driver, a chef, a personal trainer, a masseuse and a record producer are all on hand. For a longer stay, the Pages' apartment on the opposite side of the building is available. *413 Bourke Street, T 8353 8200, www.mooghotel.com*

## Blacket

Something of a find right in the heart of the city, the 42-room Blacket is housed in the former HQ of the Scottish Australia bank, dating back to the 1850s (the hotel is named after the original architect, Edmund Thomas Blacket). Some of the heritage features remain, including claw-foot baths in many of the rooms, but are set in a muted, contemporary interior. The best suites to book are the Cityscape Lofts (above), which have bedrooms on a mezzanine level and an open-plan living area below. While you're there, have a meal at the in-house Minc Restaurant (T 9279 2030), which has glimpses of the city skyline, then cosy up in the intimate Minc Lounge.

*70 King Street/George Street, T 9279 3030, www.theblacket.com*

### Regents Court

During its 16 years of operation, Regents Court has built up a huge, regular clientele. The 32 rooms, each with their own kitchen, have a chic vibe and are individually decorated with artwork and mid-century furniture collected by the owners Paula and Tom McMahon. But it's the attentive service that really appeals. Well, that and the rooftop garden (overleaf) with barbecue that overlooks the city – the perfect spot for enjoying your first coffee of the morning or a glass of wine at the day's end. Great supporters of Sydney's arts scene, the McMahons offer a residency programme for artists and writers, so you can live and work in the heart of the city for between three and 12 weeks.

*18 Springfield Avenue, T 9358 1533,*
*www.regentscourt.com.au*

## Blue

The name might have changed, but it's business as usual down by the water. Taj Hotels acquired the W Sydney in February 2006 and rebranded it Blue. The 100 rooms, such as the Wharf Room (left) although a little small,are chic and luxurious, as one would expect, and the setting – within an old finger wharf at Woolloomooloo, originally built in 1910 during the wheat and wool boom – gives the hotel its unique charm. The Atrium Bar (above), with its layabout sofas and low lighting, is the place to start and end a big evening. Great restaurants nearby include Manta (T 9322 3655) and the famous Otto (T 9368 7488), and you can relax at Spa Chakra (see p089). Russell Crowe lives in the complex at the end of the Wharf.
*6 Cowper Wharf Road, T 9331 9000, www.tajhotels.com/sydney*

Pool, Blue

### Establishment

While it might be located in the heart of the city's business district – which also means it's just a short walk to the Opera House (see p010), Circular Quay and the bars and restaurants of that area – there are enough entertainment and dining options in this hotel complex to keep most party animals happy. Owned by the Hemmes family, who run a number of Sydney's better-known bars and clubs, the hotel has a discreet entrance far removed from the bustling action in its main bar (right), which fronts onto George Street; the restaurant is run by the distinguished Peter Doyle. The hotel has 31 rooms, half with pale, calming interiors and the remainder, such as the Studio Penthouse Suite (above), with a slicker, sexier vibe – black floorboards, splashes of colour and high ceilings. Go for the latter.

*5 Bridge Lane, T 9240 3100,*
*www.merivale.com/establishment/hotel*

### Ravesi's

Throw open the balcony doors and breathe in the sea air. All but two of the 16 sophisticated rooms at Ravesi's have views of the famous Bondi Beach (see p013). But even these two smaller rooms are comfortable (and budget-priced), thanks to the 2002 renovation by the designer Dane van Bree, who avoided the often-seen, twee pale aquas for this beachfront property and opted instead for a far more masculine approach. Each of the rooms is unique, with a black, copper and bronze palette and artwork. But the main attraction has to be the Executive Split Level Suite (above) – the only one with a full frontal view of that golden stretch of sand. Step out onto the sunny balcony and check out the vista. *Campbell Parade/Hall Street, T 9365 4422, www.ravesis.com.au*

### Hilton

It was always something of an institution
but, having seen better days, the old
building in the city centre was torn down
and the new, improved Hilton opened in
July 2005. From the magnificent Bronwyn
Oliver sculpture in the towering foyer
(right) to the 500-plus rooms, this hotel
may have a big name, but it's all Sydney
style. For a designer option, book one of
the 15 Relaxation Suites (above). All are
situated at the building's corners and
spread between the 29th to 43nd floors,
so the views are amazing. Even if you
don't stay, it's worth a visit. Luke Mangan,
formerly of Salt, oversees Glass Brasserie
(T 9265 6068), the Tony Chi-designed
New York-style eaterie. The stunning
Marble Bar (T 9265 6094), built in 1893,
has an Italian Renaissance style and
Belgian, Italian and African marble walls.
*488 George Street, T 9266 2000,*
*www.hiltonsydney.com.au*

### Kirketon

We're not sure how they do it, but one of the city's most acclaimed boutique hotels was bought by new owners, Eight Hotels, in 2003 and since then the room rate has plummeted. It's still as tony as ever, with the muted minimalist rooms designed by Burley Katon Halliday in demand from fashion and film types (who we're sure are very happy with the complimentary passes for the nearby Bayswater Fitness, T 9356 2555). When you make your reservation, ask for one of the six rooms facing the road (they're a little larger than the rest) or try the Executive Room (right). The latest attraction is the new Kirketon Dining Room & Bar, run by James Ingram, formerly of the very popular International. Situated on the ground floor, it offers a French-influenced menu in an ambient low-lighting setting.
*229 Darlinghurst Road, T 9332 2011, www.kirketon.com.au*

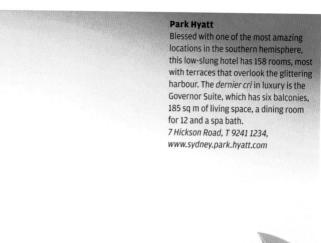

### Park Hyatt

Blessed with one of the most amazing
locations in the southern hemisphere,
this low-slung hotel has 158 rooms, most
with terraces that overlook the glittering
harbour. The *dernier cri* in luxury is the
Governor Suite, which has six balconies,
185 sq m of living space, a dining room
for 12 and a spa bath.
*7 Hickson Road, T 9241 1234,*
*www.sydney.park.hyatt.com*

### Medusa

With its scarlet exterior, you can't miss the Medusa as you stroll down Darlinghurst Road. Scott Weston's lusciously colourful design – pink in the hallway, red carpet, and lots of yellows and oranges – makes this the most individual and artistic boutique hotel in Sydney. A Darlinghurst mansion, built in the early 1900s, has been converted into 17 contemporary rooms, each one different from the rest, but all with magnificent proportions, thanks to the original building. The owners Terry and Robert Schwamberg recommend the top-floor Grand Room (above), with a view that takes in the courtyard (right), with its impressive fountain, and the city. If you should have a friend of the four-legged variety, rest easy: the ground-floor rooms cater for pooches too.

*267 Darlinghurst Road, T 9331 1000, www.medusa.com.au*

**Alba Penthouse**

One of the most recent additions to Contemporary Hotels' Apartments collection is the Alba Penthouse, situated in buzzing Surry Hills. The huge three double-bedroom apartment is spread across two levels, offering serious views of the city. This luxury pad maintains the airy dimensions of the original 1930s building, formerly a maternity hospital that was transformed into a multi-use development by architects SJB+PTW. The large terrace is the perfect place to relax, particularly after dark. Make use of the complex's pool, gym and sauna, or visit the cafés, restaurants and Object gallery (see p079) downstairs, which showcases contemporary Australian craft and design.
*437 Bourke Street, T 9331 2881,*
*www.contemporaryhotels.com.au*

# 24 HOURS
## SEE THE BEST OF THE CITY IN JUST ONE DAY

Ask 20 Sydneysiders how to spend the perfect day in their beloved city and you are sure to get 20 different responses: shopping, sunbathing on the beach, hanging out in a laid-back beer garden, checking out some of the world-class art galleries or eating until you are fit to burst. There is one thing you can be guaranteed – you won't be disappointed. If there's a cliché that sums up Sydney, it is this: there is definitely something for everyone. What you will need, if you're to sample all its delights, is an open mind, a lot of energy and a pair of shoes that isn't going to give you blisters and slow you down.

You'll want to make the most of the sunshine, the fantastic parks, the wonderful harbour, and some of the brilliant food and wine that the city is so famous for. So, get a good night's sleep (everyone needs one occasionally), then head for the beach early in the morning and fuel up at Three Eggs (opposite) before heading into the city. Here, we've put together a little culture, the Art Gallery of New South Wales (see p044), a sample of Australian flora and fauna at the Royal Botanic Gardens (see p042), some of the best antipodean cuisine at ARIA (see p043) and cocktails at the Opera Bar (see p046) and a night out, Sydney style, along Oxford Street at The Colombian Hotel (see p047), Midnight Shift (see p047) or Spectrum (see p047), or at all of them.

*For all addresses, see Resources.*

### 08.30 Three Eggs

It's time to fuel up for the day ahead, and although this local café doesn't have views of famous Bondi Beach, it's just around the corner. New owners have taken over what people familiar to the area will know as Brown Sugar and have renamed it Three Eggs, which gives you a fairly good indication of what you'll be having for breakfast. Try the goat's cheese omelette or the Parmesan scrambled eggs, with a strong coffee and fresh juice on the side, and enjoy the friendly service and relaxed atmosphere.

*100 Brighton Boulevard, T 9365 6262*

### 10.00 Royal Botanic Gardens

Located in the Domain, the area south of the Sydney Opera House (see p010), is the Royal Botanic Gardens, Australia's oldest scientific institution, founded by Governor Macquarie in 1816. It's a beautiful place for a stroll and you can find, among many other treasures, an example of the Wollemi Pine, thought to be extinct until 1994, and tropical gardens growing in the two glasshouses, one a pyramid (above). If you follow Mrs Macquaries Road down from the Art Gallery of New South Wales (see p044) and towards the harbour, you'll find the information centre where you can get a map. From the gardens it's a short stroll to the foreshore. *Mrs Macquaries Road, T 9231 8111, www.rbgsyd.nsw.gov.au*

### 12.30 Aria

Just a few minutes away is one of the city's great restaurants serving modern Australian cuisine. Matthew Moran is the head chef and co-owner of Aria, and he prides himself on bringing the best local, seasonal produce to the table. The room itself is a lesson in artful subtlety that lets the spectacular view do most of the talking. Might we suggest starting with some freshly shucked Sydney rock oysters followed by the twice cooked Bangalow sweet pork belly with caramelised apple and balsamic vinegar? If the decision is too hard, let someone else choose for you or take the option of the seven-course tasting menu with wine matches.
*1 Macquarie Street, T 9252 2555, www.ariarestaurant.com.au*

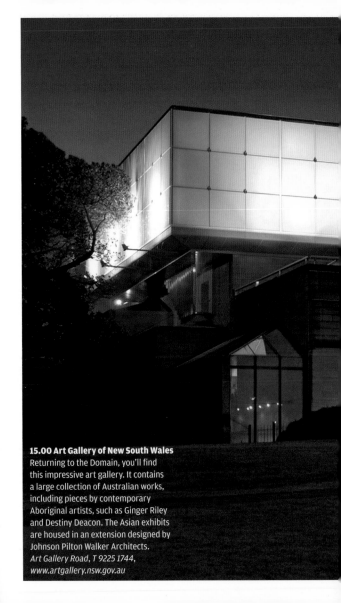

**15.00 Art Gallery of New South Wales**
Returning to the Domain, you'll find
this impressive art gallery. It contains
a large collection of Australian works,
including pieces by contemporary
Aboriginal artists, such as Ginger Riley
and Destiny Deacon. The Asian exhibits
are housed in an extension designed by
Johnson Pilton Walker Architects.
*Art Gallery Road, T 9225 1744,*
*www.artgallery.nsw.gov.au*

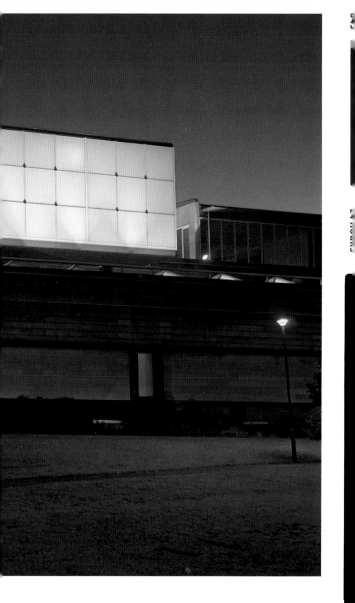

### 19.30 Opera Bar

By now, you're probably in the market for a cold drink. Watch for the crowd that gathers on the forecourt near the Sydney Opera House (see p010) and you'll have found the Opera Bar. It's an impressive destination with great views of the harbour and the city skyline, and you really can't beat snagging a table in the enormous outdoor area when the sun is shining. There's also a much smaller indoor area with booths, low-slung stools and ottomans, and this is where you'll need to go to purchase your cocktail of choice. Every day, there's live music, from jazz to funk to groovy beats. Then head over to dinner at Longrain (see p052), just a short taxi ride from the Oxford Street late night action.
*Lower Concourse Level, Sydney Opera House, T 9247 1666, www.operabar.com.au*

## 22.30 Oxford Street

If Disneyland is the happiest place on earth, then Oxford Street, Darlinghurst after 10pm is definitely the gayest place on earth, plus there's as much neon as Disney's Main Street Electrical Parade and almost as many tourists. The street itself, is a little down at heel but was undergoing major upgrades as we went to press. You'll see the rainbow flag outside many bars. The Colombian Hotel (T 9360 2151, above), with its über-camp tropical decor, is a great drinking hole, where the window seats in the downstairs bar are the place to be. If you want to dance, particularly among men with no shirts on, head to Midnight Shift (T 9360 4319), one of Sydney's longest running gay clubs. If not, check out Spectrum (see p049), an indie joint with up-and-coming bands and club nights.

# URBAN LIFE
## CAFÉS, RESTAURANTS, BARS AND NIGHTCLUBS

Sydneysiders have a reputation for being somewhat, well, fickle. 'If you open, they will come' is the mantra. The problem is, they may only come for a couple of weeks before moving on to the next big thing. That's not to say that all new establishments disappear as quickly as they bloom, but what it does mean is that when a place is a stayer, it really is good. While the city has its share of big-budget interiors, some of the best nights are to be found in low-key spots frequented by inner-city locals, such as the Darlo Bar (Darlinghurst Road/Liverpool Street, T 9331 3672), where pretty girls and cool guys lounge on second-hand furniture and sip cold beers. The Civic (Pitt Street/Goulburn Street, T 8080 7000), which has an art deco interior, guarantees a lively evening on a Saturday, with music supplied by well-known spinners.

It is hard to say what nights are best when it comes to other bars and clubs. One Thursday somewhere will be pumping and the next week it'll be dead. The only general rule you can apply is that if the first bar you go to is quiet, it's going to be a slow night almost everywhere. A couple of things to remember: smoking is banned inside all restaurants (and in some bars and, increasingly, pubs) and BYO means 'bring your own' – wine, that is. These are some of our favourite spots to dine, drink and dance, old and new, covering the spectrum, from sophisticated to relaxed.

*For all addresses, see Resources.*

### Spectrum

This great little club, a hit with indie kids, seems a little out of place on Sydney's gay strip, Oxford Street. Holding only slightly more than 200 punters, it is one of the city's best spots to catch bands on the verge and, when they've packed up their amps for the evening, it's the turn of the DJs who are more likely to play guitar pop and rock than anything that could be categorised by its bpm.

And it is far more stylish than your average band venue, with artworks by Mathias Gerber, the brother of one of the owners, livening up the walls. There's no telephone, but you can visit the website (below) to see what's coming up, or grab a copy of *Drum Media*, the most popular of Sydney's free music mags, to check out Spectrum's listing. *34 Oxford Street, www.pashpresents.com*

### The Fringe

With a more eclectic, bohemian vibe since February 2006, this reliable venue still has friendly bar folk who can mix a demon cocktail and, thanks to great DJs on the decks, everyone is here to have fun. Monday's comedy night has been reinstated and The Fringe is now open until 3am, Thursday to Saturday.
*106 Oxford Street. T 9360 5443, www.thefringe.com.au*

### Longrain

Many a Wallpaper* staffer passing through
Sydney has made like a local here, drinking
far too many stick drinks while waiting for
a table to become available. Longrain
opened in 1999, in a converted warehouse,
with three massive communal tables
running through it, and has been packing
people in ever since. Executive chef Martin
Boetz's food is modern Thai/Asian-inspired
and it's best to come with a group so you
can order as many of the generous dishes
on his menu as possible. While everything
is beyond fantastic, do not – we repeat,
do not – leave without trying the crispy
skin Barossa chicken with a spiced blood-
plum sauce, or the caramelised pork hock
with five-spice and chilli vinegar. It should
be illegal to visit Sydney and not come
to Longrain. Bear in mind there is a
no-reservations policy for dinner.
*85 Commonwealth Street, T 9280 2888,*
*www.longrain.com.*

### Fratelli Paradiso

In the morning, they arrive for espresso and pastries; in the evening, the local crowd clusters for the ever-changing Italian classics listed on the blackboard. Brothers Giovanni and Enrico Paradiso have turned a small bakery and bistro into a destination for great food and a laid-back atmosphere, particularly for those regular customers who are always remembered and treated like long-lost friends. A talking point is the fantastic custom-designed wallpaper featuring Rolling Stones-esque lips slurping up spaghetti. Make sure you order the only dish that never comes off the menu: *calamari Sant'Andrea* – lightly battered calamari served on a rocket salad with balsamic dressing. *12 Challis Avenue, T 9357 1744*

## Lotus Bar

The fresh, funky bistro out front is a great place to stop for a bite to eat, but when you're sated head back to the bar, a den of exotica, with snakeskin walls on one side and metallic wallpaper on the other. The candlelight is oh-so low that making eye contact across the tiny room is almost impossible. Behind the bar, Alexx Swainston is a complete gem. If you can't be bothered to consult the seven-page drinks list, she'll concoct something for you based on the time of day, the mood you're in or even on whether you've eaten or not. That said, you really shouldn't miss the Detox Julep – a blend of fresh mint, pineapple chunks, vanilla sugar, fresh ginger and Bison grass vodka, A$16.
*22 Challis Avenue, T 9326 9000,*
*www.merivale.com/lotus/bar*

### North Bondi Italian Food

It's a case of share and share alike at the north end of Bondi, where – not satisfied with already having the best venue in the area (the Icebergs Dining Room and Bar, see p062) – Maurice Terzini and chef Robert Marchetti have taken over the space underneath the North Bondi RSL Club (T 9130 3152). Order plates of roast suckling meats, calamari, baccalà (salted cod) balls and Italian cheeses, then place them in the middle of the table, so everyone gets a taste. The vibe is casual in this trattoria-style venue, but it's still as cool as, well, Icebergs. Arrive early (or hold out for a late supper), as there is a no-reservations policy.
*120 Ramsgate Avenue, T 9300 4400, www.idrb.com*

### Cafe Sopra

Downstairs is one of the city's favourite providores, Fratelli Fresh (T 1300 552 119), while upstairs, past the tins of Italian tomatoes and packets of pasta, is a simple café-style venue that keeps locals happy at breakfast and for lunch. Chef Andy Bunn sends out simple, Italian food, such as lightly fried zucchini flowers, stuffed with five Italian cheeses, ox-heart tomato salad, panini and mouth-watering pasta (look out for the lamb ragu). The staff here are efficient and friendly, even during the busiest times. If there are no tables, take a seat at the long bar.
*7 Danks Street, T 9699 3174*

## Coast

On a sunny afternoon, you couldn't find a more beautiful place to indulge than the reopened Coast. The huge room is glass on three sides, opening on to an enormous wooden deck that overlooks Darling Harbour. Inside, the design by Hassell Architects and Frost Design is strikingly simple, with a yellow light installation running the length of the room suggesting the Australian coastline.

Stefano Manfredi, one of the city's best-loved chefs, serves up Italian cuisine to match the setting. Any order should include a selection of freshly shucked oysters, the salumi platter and the barbecued whole rabbit. At night, when the harbour lights up, you'll be treated to the view of a lifetime.

*The Roof Terrace, Cockle Bay Wharf, T 9267 6700, www.coastrestaurant.com.au*

**Ruby Rabbit**
There is nothing average about this inimate two-storey club, with the decor designed by co-owner Phil Schell. Inside you'll find bespoke wallpaper in a rainbow of hues, 1960s burnt orange tiles, a baby grand piano and 108 free-hanging bulbs. Visiting rock 'dignitaries' flock here, and the entertainment ranges from DJs to visual installations. *231 Oxford Street, T 9326 0044*

**Icebergs Dining Room and Bar**
When paparazzi shots of visiting movie
stars and singers appear in the local
newpapers, the celebs in question have
invariably been caught outside this venue,
which was designed by Italian architect
Claudio Lazzarini and Australian architect
Carl Pickering. Lots of attention has been
paid to this prime piece of real estate,
opened in 2002 and run by restaurateur
Maurice Terzini, not least because of its
enviable position perched high over the
southern end of Bondi Beach (see p013).
This is one of the coolest places in the city
to sup, while the restaurant, which serves
modern Mediterranean fare, with an
emphasis on seafood, is first-class. You can
hardly go wrong with the extensive wine
list, either. Go on a week night when it's a
little quieter, and hang out with the locals
having cocktails in the chi-chi bar.
*1 Notts Avenue, T 9365 9000,*
*www.idrb.com*

### Billy Kwong

The only bad thing about this relaxed affair, which is run by chef Kylie Kwong (who, since she opened this restaurant six years ago, has hit television screens and put her name to a number of books) is that you can't reserve a table. No fear: give the floor staff your mobile number, have a drink across the road at the Dolphin Hotel (T 9331 4800) and wait for a spot to open up. It's worth the wait for Kwong's take on her mother's traditional recipes, cooked with the best organic and biodynamic produce available. Try the crispy-skin duck with blood-plum sauce. *355 Crown Street, T 9332 3300*

### The Loft

For those who prefer comfort and
sophistication, this venue offers an
opulent Middle Eastern feel. Ask for
a table next to the windows so that
you can see the view of Darling Harbour.
Sunday evenings see DJs, musicians
and filmmakers doing their thing at
'Freeform – Freestyle Sunday Sessions'.
*3 Lime Street, King Street Wharf,*
*T 9299 4770, www.theloftsydney.com*

## YU

Probably the best-looking club in the
city, thanks to its 2000 refit by architect
Paul Kelly. Sunday's After Ours (www.
afterours.com) is huge, with two rooms
of music kicking on until 6am; Friday is
house night; and Saturday is a mixed
feast of parties. If you must, escape the
noise at the chic Soho Bar upstairs.
*171 Victoria Street, T 9358 6511,*
*www.yu.com.au*

# INSIDER'S GUIDE

## EVA GALAMBOS, BOUTIQUE OWNER

Eva Galambos divides her time between two of Sydney's best-known neighbourhoods. She was born and raised in Bondi and still lives there, while her recently revamped, glamorous store Parlour X (213 Glenmore Road, T 9331 0999) is located at Fiveways in Paddington, which boasts lots of chi-chi shops, art galleries and markets (held on Saturdays). For a glitzy night out, she says you can't beat drinks at the seriously A-list Hemmesphere (252 George Street, T 9240 3000), a small Moroccan-themed space upstairs at Establishment (see p026).

For a breakfast, lunch or dinner that's a little more relaxed, Local Wine Bar & Restaurant (211 Glenmore Road, T 9332 1577), just a few doors down from Parlour X, serves great bistro food and has a lovely, leafy courtyard that will make you wish you were a local, too. Lovers of Japanese food should visit the funky Rise (23 Craigend Street, T 9357 1755). Not only are the dining room and food divine, but each morsel from the seven-course *omakase* (degustation) menu looks as if it has been styled for a magazine. At any time of the day, Galambos likes to visit the Tropicana Caffe (227 Victoria Street, T 9360 9809), a Sydney institution frequented by a cross-section of the community, from lawyers to graphic designers and students, who spill out onto tables on the Darlinghurst footpath. It's not fancy, but the coffee and people-watching prospects are good.

# ARCHITOUR

## A GUIDE TO SYDNEY'S ICONIC BUILDINGS

Just over 311 years have elapsed since it was colonised, and Sydney does not have the diverse architectural offerings of many cities its size. What it does have, however, are some very interesting examples of art deco, modernist and contemporary buildings, designed by both Australian and overseas architects. In a city that prides itself on having one of the most beautiful harbours in the world, it should come as no surprise that much of the interest in development and redevelopment hangs around the water. For many, it causes concern and controversy – after all, it doesn't take a rocket scientist to realise that water views and private jetties equal megabucks for property developers, yet many community activists envisage important harbour sites being reclaimed for public use as parks, and recreational and cultural areas.

So, you have areas where important historical buildings, such as those located on wharves in the inner harbour that serve as reminders of the city's maritime past, are being rescued, while others are being visually vandalised. Take, for example, the apartment blocks built on East Circular Quay at the end of the 2::1s – dubbed 'the Toaster' by locals – that block views to the Sydney Opera House (see p121). Here, we take a tour of the more notable examples of Sydney architecture – some highly visible and others a little harder to find, though no less interesting.

*For all addresses, see Resources.*

### Sydney Theatre

In this theatre, opened in 2004, architect Andrew Andersons impressively marries modern design (in the asymmetrical foyer and in the slender balcony that overlooks the street) to the heritage elements of an old bond store, including restored walls of convict-hewn cliff faces (in the backstage area). For the audience, there are 850 seats covered in a purple stretch fabric rather than the standard velvet. Andrew Andersons' firm, Peddle Thorp & Walker, also designed the Hickson Road Bistro (T 9250 1990) next door. A stunning red glass screen marks the transition between the two spaces.

*22 Hickson Road, T 9250 1900, www.sydneytheatre.org.au*

**Castlecrag and Middle Harbour houses**
Contemporaries of Frank Lloyd Wright, Walter Burley Griffin and his wife Marion came to Australia from the USA in 1914, after winning a competition to design the nation's capital, Canberra. When things didn't go to plan – bureaucrats and the First World War among the obstacles – they decided to adapt their principles to a large parcel of land in the Castlecrag area. There are 16 Griffin buildings situated on Edinburgh Road: The Parapet and The Barbette (including the Castlecrag Private Hospital at number 150), which were all built between 1921 and 1924. In the same area are houses by Neville Gruzman (17 North Arm Road) and Hugh Buhrich (375 Edinburgh Road, right). Although not open to the public, many of these buildings are visible from the street. Graham Jahn's *Guide to Sydney Architecture* (Watermark Press) has a map that you can follow.

### Rose Seidler House

The house that Harry Seidler, one of Australia's most famous architects and an émigré from Vienna, built for his mother in 1950 is possibly the best-preserved example of modernist architecture in the country. The elevated, cubiform house is arranged in a U shape around an outdoor terrace (featuring a mural by Seidler) and explores the relationship between indoor and outdoor spaces using glass walls fitted with timber frames that overlook the neighbouring national park. All of the original appliances remain in the kitchen, and the other rooms are furnished with pieces by Eames, Saarinen and the like. Now under the care of the Historic Houses Trust, the house is open each Sunday from 10am to 5pm. It's 30km north of the city. *71 Clissold Road, Wahroonga, T 9989 8020, www.hht.net.au/museums*

**Museum of Contemporary Art**

Originally the offices for the Maritime Services Board, this prominent H-shaped art deco building, on the waterfront at West Circular Quay, became Australia's leading gallery for contemporary art at the end of 1991. Despite extensive internal remodelling to house the various galleries, the exterior of local sandstone with granite detailing remains largely as it was, designed by two government architects, WH Withers and WDH Baxter, in the 1940s. In the foyer, the floor is made of marble extracted near Goulburn, edged with green marble from Mudgee, overlooked by a mezzanine balcony with a wave-design balustrade. One of the most popular exhibitions is 'Primavera', which showcases young artists each year.
*140 George Street, T 9245 2400, www.mca.com.au*

### Object

After temporarily being without a home, Object gallery reopened in July 2004 as part of the mixed-use St Margarets development in Surry Hills. The circular building, the former hospital chapel designed by Ken Woolley in 1955, has been remodelled by architect Sam Marshall to suit its new function: that of displaying contemporary craft and design. The walls of the original double-height design consist of a staggered circle of concrete panels, connected by glass slots that allow natural light to flood the building. Some of the chapel's features have been maintained, while other elements, such as a mezzanine gallery space, have been added. Entry is through a hall consisting of coloured glass panels.
*415 Bourke Street, T 9361 4555,*
*www.object.com.au*

# SHOPPING

## THE CITY'S FINEST SHOPS (AND WHAT TO BUY)

From huge, faceless malls covering more acreage than any person could possibly manage in a day, to quirky neighbourhood streets lined with unique boutiques, Sydney can give your credit cards a complete workout. For those who want to shop all day, there is no denying the lure of Oxford Street, Paddington, where you can flick through tomes about art and design at Ariel Books (42 Oxford Street, T 9332 4581) or try on perfume and make-up at Mecca Cosmetica (126 Oxford Street, T 9361 4488). Stores showcasing some of Australia's more established designers, including Scanlan & Theodore (122 Oxford Street, T 9380 9388), Zimmermann (24 Oxford Street, T 9360 5769) and Von Troska (294 Oxford Street, T 9360 7522), are also here, while forays down side streets will take you to Collette Dinnigan (33 William Street, T 9360 6691), Leona Edmiston (88 William Street, T 9331 7033) and Akira Isogawa (12a Queen Street, T 9361 5221).

Of the more interesting department stores, search out David Jones. Its two largest locations, in the CBD (86-108 Castlereagh Street, T 9266 5544) and Bondi Junction (500 Oxford Street, T 9619 1111), stock just about everything by local and international designers. And then there are the markets, the perfect place to fair-weather shop. The largest is the Paddington Bazaar (St John's Church, Oxford Street, T 9331 2646), held on Saturdays.

*For all addresses, see Resources.*

## Planet

Ross Longmuir first dreamed up the idea for Planet in Melbourne, but eight years ago he relocated to this smart store in the heartland of Surry Hills. Longmuir's own clean, modern furniture designs are displayed alongside studio ceramics, textiles and other homewares made by contemporary Australian designers and artists – all from local raw materials. Among the highlights, and there are many, are the delicate porcelain cups by ceramicist Ruth McMillan, from A$50, Robin Best's amazing 'Marine Series' porcelain vases and bowls that she engraves with a jeweller's tool, from A$2,200, and Barbara Rogers' textile designs that are made employing Japanese Shibori techniques.

*419 Crown Street, T 9698 0680,*
*www.planetfurniture.com.au*

### Di Croco

While most of the skins from Australian saltwater crocodiles are shipped overseas for use by companies such as Hermès, there is one local company making luxury goods from this scary creature. Heather Brown launched Di Croco in 1998 and began making handbags, shoes, belts and other accessories in a range of styles and colours. In October 2005, she opened a small outlet in Sydney, which has already become a firm favourite among well-heeled locals and international visitors looking for something unique to take back home. The store itself, designed by Paul Jones and Associates, is beautiful too and features cabinetry made from New Guinea rosewood and doors inlaid with Australian saltwater crocodile skin.
*7 Bay Street, T 9362 4678,*
*www.dicroco.com.au*

WARNING
24 HOUR VIDEO
SURVEILLANCE
IN OPERATION

### Cloth

Having outgrown its original beachside home, Julie Paterson moved her small business producing hand screen-printed fabrics on hemp and linen to a larger store in Randwick. Paterson's designs start as paintings on wood and are then developed further before being printed off-site in a tin shed in rural New South Wales. Some of her more contemporary designs – 'pickupsticks' and 'stuffed olives' (from A$132 per sq m), for instance – are now being made by a much bigger company, Woven Image (T 9326 0433), on a heavy-duty linen and cotton base. At the store, as well as buying bolts of fabric, you can purchase a range of clothing, table and bed linen, cushions, lampshades, and a new range of rugs. *54a Carrington Road, T 9326 7755, www.clothfabric.com*

### Wheels & Doll Baby

Its slogan 'Clothes to snare a millionaire' has tempted such international hotties as Kate Moss, Gwen Stefani and Deborah Harry. Dita Von Teese is the latest star to be caught wearing the sassy, 1950s-inspired designs by Melanie Greensmith. When she opened this store in 1987, Greensmith sold hard-to-find imports from the UK and US. But she soon found she had a designer's touch and has never looked back. From flirty ra-ra skirts to milkmaid tops and sexy dresses trimmed with diamanté, this is fashion that never goes out of fashion. She also has a decently organised online store.
*259 Crown Street, T 9361 3286, www.wheelsanddollbaby.com*

## Space Furniture

This mega designer furniture store first opened in Sydney in 1993 and quickly established itself as the place to buy the chicest elements for the home. In May 2004, it relocated to a new six-level showroom designed by Nik Karalis of Woods Bagot Architects – he also designed the Brisbane (T 07 3253 6000) and Singapore (T 00 65 6415 0000) stores. Put the 4,000 sq m interior to good use and lounge around trying out the ranges by B&B Italia, Kartell, Cassina, Edra and Zanotta. Also, marvel at the expressive lighting designs by Ingo Maurer and pick over the extensive range of homewares and gifts – the amazing 'Melissa Scarfun' shoes by Alexandre Herchcovitch, from A$139, caught our eye. You'll also find, on site, the only Philippe Starck store in the world.
*84 O'Riordan Street, T 8339 7588, www.spacefurniture.com.au*

# SPORTS AND SPAS
## WORK OUT, CHILL OUT OR JUST WATCH

It's no secret that Australians love sport, and the facilities in the city, particularly post-Olympics, are second to none. There are gyms and public swimming pools in most suburbs, and plenty of places to train if, like many people, you fancy getting sweaty outdoors. What people thought might be a fad when boot camps started appearing about five years ago is still one of the most popular ways to train. What does it involve? Usually a picturesque beachside location, a trainer yelling demands and a group of keen people getting down and dirty at the crack of dawn. Ask a local gym – such as one in the Fitness First chain (www.fitnessfirst.com.au) – if they know where you can join a group.

For people who simply can't stand the thought of hundreds of push-ups, there's the lazy option: becoming a spectator. Sydney follows these basic rules: summer means cricket and winter brings football in its three local codes – rugby league, rugby union and Australian Rules. Although it's thought of as a Melbourne sport, with the home team, the Sydney Swans, winning the 2005 AFL premiership, the game is sure to soar to even greater heights. It's fast, it's hard and you'll need a local to explain the rules to you. Keep an eye out for matches being held at the Sydney Cricket Ground (Moore Park Road, T 9360 6601). To buy tickets, visit www.ticketek.com.au or www.ticketmaster.com.

*For all addresses, see Resources.*

## Spa Chakra

As well as being one of the best spas in the country, Chakra is also a medi-spa, which means that its therapists can provide medical and wellness care. The setting – it's located in the hotel Blue (see p022) – on one of the restored finger wharves in Woolloomooloo, is stunning, as are the clean-lined white treatment rooms. There are more than 20 treatments on offer, and Guerlain products are used in the spa. If you're feeling a little worse for wear after a long flight, ask for a package of treatments to be devised to revive you. The Energetic Massage, which removes blockages in the body caused by stress, or a pedicure (in one of the chairs, above) sound like great ways to start your trip.
*6 Cowper Wharf Road, T 9368 0888, www.spachakra.com*

**North Sydney Olympic Pool**
Since it opened in 1936, 86 world
swimming records have been set at
this pool, which has one of the most
amazing settings in the world. The
site was originally where much of the
building work for the Sydney Harbour
Bridge (see p014) took place. Today, you
can admire the results between laps.
*4 Alfred Street South, T 9955 2309,
www.northsydney.nsw.gov.au*

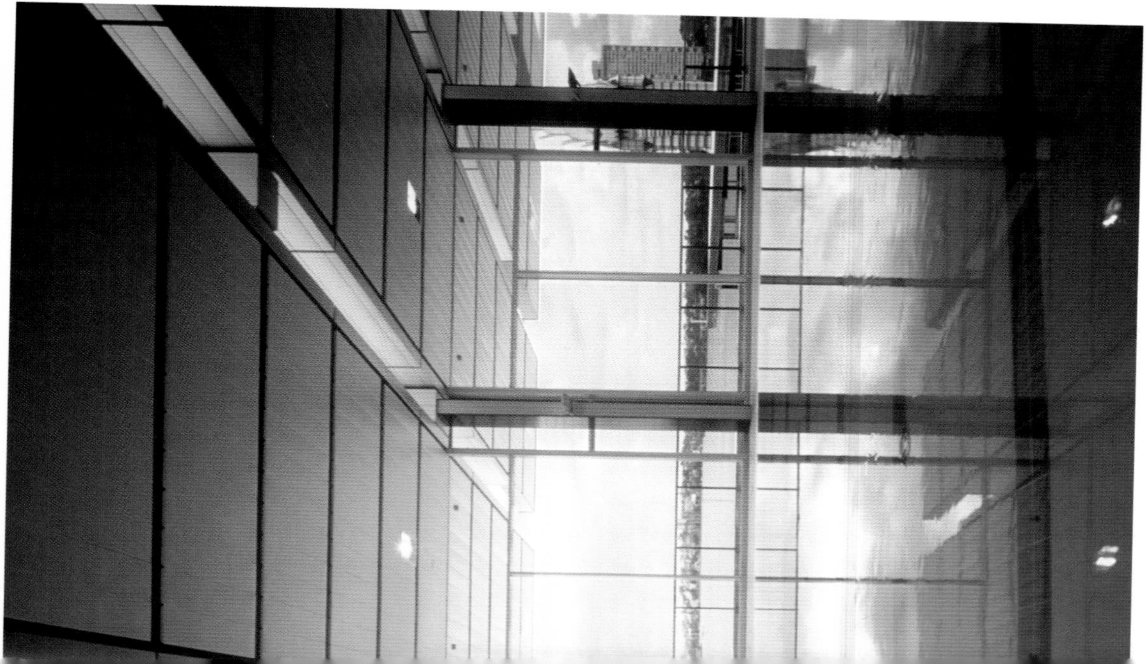

### King George V Recreation Centre

The site of this centre may be quite historic – it has been a sports venue since the 1920s – but Lippmann Associates' design for this recreation centre, opened in 1998, is nothing but contemporary with its curved steel structure. Inside, there is a fitness centre with classes from yoga to cardio-boxing, and courts for basketball, netball, volleyball and badminton, while outside there are basketball half-courts, tennis courts and a barbecue area. As well as being a sports centre for local residents and city workers, it is also something of a community social centre hosting regular barbecues and art classes.
*Cumberland Street, T 9244 3600*

### City Gym

This is the gym by which all others in the city are measured. It's huge, has been in operation for more than 25 years and has the largest free-weight station in Sydney. There is also an enviable timetable of classes, whether you're into yoga and Pilates or the action of aerobics, pump and fight-do.
*107-113 Crown Street, T 9360 6247, www.citygym.com.au*

# ESCAPES

## WHERE TO GO IF YOU WANT TO LEAVE TOWN

While you'll probably never find yourself bored when you visit Sydney, if you're here for an extended period it's worth jumping in a car and exploring some more out-of-the-way places. Just north, in fact not even really out of Sydney, is the divine beachside suburb of Palm Beach, with the Pacific Ocean on one side and Pittwater, a tranquil body of water bordering the Ku-ring-gai Chase National Park, on the other. It's a low-key playground for the rich and famous during the summer and the perfect spot to relax at any time of year. Palm Beach is about a 45-minute drive north from the city, but the most spectacular way to get there is by seaplane with Sydney By Seaplane (www.sydneybyseaplane.com), which also offers scenic and picnic flights. If it all looks a little familiar, it's because television soapie *Home and Away* is filmed locally.

A little further away is the Hunter Valley, a premium wine-growing region, two hours' drive north-west of Sydney. It really is the place for lovers of good wine and food, where you can visit the vineyards and taste the merchandise. Check out the Semillon at Brokenwood (401-427 McDonalds Road, Pokolbin, T 4998 7559), McWilliam's Mount Pleasant Estate (Marrowbone Road, Pokolbin, T 4998 7505) or the Small Winemakers Centre (426 McDonalds Road, Pokolbin, T 4998 7668). If you're really keen, visit the area's wine tourism website at www.winecountry.com.au.

*For all addresses, see Resources.*

### Palm Beach

As they say, when in Rome... The beach at Palmie (as Sydneysiders call it) sees miles of golden sand stretched out in both directions. Grab a towel, find a great spot and lie around, soak up the sun and enjoy the most pleasurable of pastimes: watching the parade of surfers and other beachgoers. It's uphill all the way, but make sure you do the 40-minute walk from Governor Phillip Park to the Barrenjoey Lighthouse. From up here, in the Ku-ring-gai Chase National Park, you can see all across Pittwater and along the coast. Pittwater is also a great spot for trying sailing or windsurfing, particularly if you've never had a go before. You can hire all the gear as well as take a few lessons at Palm Beach Water Sports (T 0408 862 000). If you plan to stay the night, book in at Jonah's (T 9974 5599).

### Tonic, Hunter Valley
How can you resist the charms of one of the region's newest boutique hotel options? Tonic (right) has just eight rooms with not a jot of chintz. It's a steel and glass design with polished concrete floors, cowhide rugs and valley views. Also, try Shakey Tables (T 4938 1744), an eclectic, quirky restaurant.
*251 Talga Road, Lovedale, T 4930 9999, www.tonichotel.com.au*

## Huski

Should the sun and sea get too much, the Australian Alps are one option. The region's Mount Hotham Airport is just 85 minutes from Sydney. Twenty minutes from there, within the ski resort of Falls Creek, lies Huski. The look of this impressive boutique apartment block, designed by Melbourne architects Elenberg Fraser, is as far from the traditional Alpine chalet as you can get. The design was inspired by the random angles of snowflake segments. There are just 14 apartments — from studios (with a spa in the bathroom instead of a balcony jacuzzi) to duplex penthouses sleeping up to 10 people — all finished with modern, custom-made furnishings and featuring 120-degree sweeping views. During the ski season (June to October), no cars are allowed in the village.

*Sitzmark Street, Falls Creek, Victoria,*
*T 1300 652 260, www.huski.com.au*

## Blue Mountains

If the hustle of Sydney gets too much, head for the hills. An hour by car or train is a string of quaint villages, high in the Blue Mountains (www.bluemts.com.au). The landscape is astonishing and when you are overlooking craggy Three Sisters it's easy to forget the city is so close. Check in to the elegant Echoes Boutique Hotel and Restaurant in Katoomba (T 4782 1966) and have a drink in the Mercure Grand Hydro Majestic hotel (T 4788 1002).

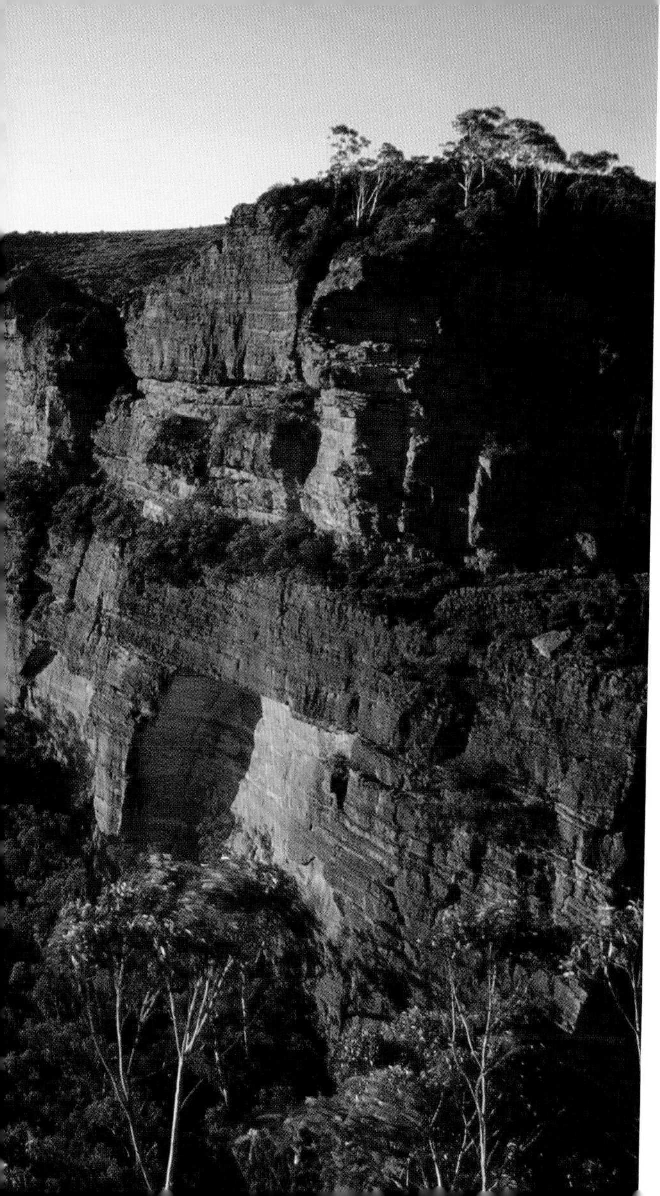

# NOTES
**SKETCHES AND MEMOS**

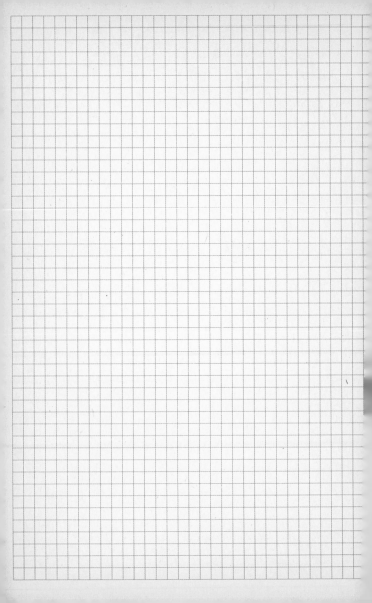

# RESOURCES
## ADDRESSES AND ROOM RATES

### LANDMARKS
**009 Horizon**
*184 Forbes Street*
**009 Skywalk**
*Centrepoint Podium Level*
*100 Market Street*
*T 9333 9222*
*www.skywalk.com.au*
**009 Sydney Tower**
*100 Market Street*
**009 Taronga Zoo**
*Bradleys Head Road*
*T 9969 2777*
*www.zoo.nsw.gov.au*
**010 Sydney Opera House**
*Bennelong Point*
*T 9250 7111*
*www.sydneyopera*
*house.com*
**012 Aurora Place**
*88 Phillip Street*
*T 8243 4400*
*www.auroraplace.com.au*
**013 Bondi Surf Bathers'**
**Life Saving Club**
*Queen Elizabeth Drive*
*T 9300 9279*
*www.bondisurfclub.com*
**014 BridgeClimb**
*Sydney Harbour Bridge*
*T 8274 7777*
*www.bridgeclimb.com*

### HOTELS
**016 Four Seasons at**
**The Rocks**
Room rates:
double, A$350–A$470
*199 George Street*
*T 9238 0000*
*www.fourseasons.com*
**016 Sheraton On**
**The Park**
Room rates:
double, A$590
*161 Elizabeth Street*
*T 9286 6000*
*www.sheratonhotels.com*
**017 Mooghotel**
Room rates:
double, A$990
*413 Bourke Street*
*T 8353 8200*
*www.mooghotel.com*
**018 Blacket**
Room rates:
double, A$210;
Cityscape Loft, A$325
*70 King Street/*
*George Street*
*T 9279 3030*
*www.theblacket.com*
**018 Minc Restaurant**
*Level 3*
*70 King Street/*
*George Street*
*T 9279 2030*
*www.theblacket.com*
**019 Regents Court**

Room rates:
double, A$240
*18 Springfield Avenue*
*T 9358 1533*
*www.regentscourt.com.au*
**022 Blue**
Room rates:
double, A$355
*6 Cowper Wharf Road*
*T 9331 9000*
*www.tajhotels.com/sydney*
**022 Manta**
*Cowper Wharf Roadway*
*T 9322 3655*
*www.mantarestaurant.*
*com.au*
**022 Otto Ristorante**
**Italiano**
*Area 8*
*6 Cowper Wharf Road*
*T 9368 7488*
*www.ottoristorante.*
*com.au*
**026 Establishment**
Room rates:
double, A$350;
Studio Penthouse
Suite, A$970
*5 Bridge Lane*
*T 9240 3100*
*www.merivale.com/*
*establishment/hotel*

**028 Ravesi's**
Room rates:
double, from A$125;
suite, A$450
*Campbell Parade/Hall
Street*
*T 9365 4422*
*www.ravesis.com.au*

**030 Hilton**
Room rates:
double, A$270-A$355;
Relaxation Suite, A$615
*488 George Street*
*T 9266 2000*
*www.hiltonsydney.com.au*

**030 Glass Brasserie**
*Level 2*
*488 George Street*
*T 9265 6068*
*www.glassbrasserie.
com.au*

**030 Marble Bar**
*Level B1*
*488 George Street*
*T 9265 6094*
*www.marblebar
sydney.com.au*

**032 Kirkton**
Room rates:
double, A$139-A$145
*229 Darlinghurst Road*
*T 9332 2011*
*www.kirkton.com.au*

**032 Bayswater Fitness**
*32 Bayswater Road*
*T 9356 2555*
*www.baywaters
fitness.com.au*

**034 Park Hyatt**
Room rates:
double, A$720;
Governor Suite, A$6,200
*7 Hickson Road*
*T 9241 1234*
*www.sydney.park.
hyatt.com*

**036 Medusa**
Room rates:
double, A$270;
Grand Room, A$385
*267 Darlinghurst Road*
*T 9331 1000*
*www.medusa.com.au*

**038 Alba Penthouse**
Room rates:
double, A$600-A$700
*437 Bourke Street*
*T 9331 2881*
*www.contemporary
hotels.com.au*

## 24 HOURS
**041 Three Eggs**
*100 Brighton Boulevard*
*T 9365 6262*

**042 Royal Botanic
Gardens**
*Mrs Macquaries Road*
*T 9231 8111*
*www.rbgsyd.nsw.gov.au*

**043 Aria**
*1 Macquarie Street*
*T 9252 2555*
*www.ariarestaurant.
com.au*

**044 Art Gallery of New**

South Wales
*Art Gallery Road*
*T 9225 1744*
*www.artgallery.nsw.gov.au*

**046 Opera Bar**
*Lower Concourse Level
Sydney Opera House*
*T 9247 1666*
*www.operabar.com.au*

**047 The Colombian
Hotel**
*117 Oxford Street*
*T 9360 2151*
*www.colombian.com.au*

**047 Midnight Shift**
*85 Oxford Street*
*T 9360 4319*
*www.themidnightshift.com*

## URBAN LIFE
**048 Darlo Bar**
*Darlinghurst Road/
Liverpool Street*
*T 9331 3672*
*www.darlobar.com*

**048 The Civic**
*Pitt Street/Goulburn Street*
*T 8080 7000*
*www.civichotel.com.au*

**049 Spectrum**
*34 Oxford Street*
*www.pashpresents.com*

**050 The Fringe**
*106 Oxford Street*
*T 9360 5443*
*www.thefringe.com.au*

**052 Longrain**
*85 Commonwealth Street*

T 9280 2888
www.longrain.com
**054 Fratelli Paradiso**
12 Challis Avenue
T 9357 1744
**055 Lotus Bar**
22 Challis Avenue
T 9326 9000 .
www.merivale.com
**056 North Bondi Italian Food**
120 Ramsgate Avenue
T 9300 4400
www.idrb.com
**056 North Bondi RSL Club**
118-120 Ramsgate Ave
T 9130 3152
www.northbondirsl.com.au
**058 Cafe Sopra**
7 Danks Street
T 9699 3174
**058 Fratelli Fresh**
7 Danks Street
T 1300 552 119
**059 Coast**
The Roof Terrace
Cockle Bay Wharf
T 9267 6700
www.coastrestaurant.com.au
**060 Ruby Rabbit**
231 Oxford Street
T 9326 0044
**062 Icebergs Dining Room and Bar**

I Notts Avenue
T 9365 9000
www.idrb.com
**064 Billy Kwong**
355 Crown Street
T 9332 3300
**064 The Dolphin on Crown Hotel**
412 Crown Street
T 9331 4800
**066 The Loft**
3 Lime Street
King Street Wharf
T 9299 4770
www.theloftsydney.com
**068 YU**
171 Victoria Street
T 9358 6511
www.yu.com.au
**068 Soho Bar**
171 Victoria Street
T 9358 6511
www.sohobar.com.au
**070 Hemmesphere**
252 George Street
T 9240 3000
**070 Local Wine Bar & Restaurant**
211 Glenmore Road
T 9332 1577
**070 Parlour X**
213 Glenmore Road
T 9331 0999
**070 Rise**
23 Craigend Street
T 9357 1755
**070 Tropicana Caffe**
227 Victoria Street

T 9360 9809
www.tropicanacaffe.com

## ARCHITOUR
**073 Sydney Theatre**
22 Hickson Road
T 9250 1900
www.sydneytheatre.org.au
**073 Hickson Road Bistro**
22 Hickson Road
T 9250 1900
www.sydneytheatre.org.au
**076 Rose Seidler House**
71 Clissold Road
Wahroonga
T 9989 8020
www.hht.net.au/museums
**078 Museum of Contemporary Art**
140 George Street
T 9245 2400
www.mca.com.au
**079 Object**
415 Bourke Street
T 9361 4555
www.object.com.au

## SHOPPING
**080 Akira Isogawa**
12a Queen Street
T 9361 5221
www.akira.com.au
**080 Ariel Books**
42 Oxford Street
T 9332 4581
www.arielbooks.com.au

**080 Collette Dinnigan**
*33 William Street*
*T 9360 6691*
*www.collettedinnigan.*
*com.au*

**080 David Jones**
*86-108 Castlereagh Street*
*T 9266 5544*
*500 Oxford Street*
*T 9619 1111*
*www.davidjones.com.au*

**080 Leona Edmiston**
*88 William Street*
*T 9331 7033*

**080 Mecca Cosmetica**
*126 Oxford Street*
*T 9361 4488*
*www.meccacosmetica.*
*com.au*

**080 Paddington Bazaar**
*St John's Church*
*Oxford Street*
*T 9331 2646*

**080 Scanlan & Theodore**
*122 Oxford St*
*T 9380 9388*
*www.scanlantheodore.*
*com.au*

**080 Von Troska**
*294 Oxford St*
*T 9360 7522*
*www.vontroska.com.au*

**080 Zimmermann**
*24 Oxford St*
*T 9360 5769*
*www.zimmermann*
*wear.com*

**081 Planet**
*419 Crown Street*
*T 9698 0680*
*www.planetfurniture.*
*com.au*

**082 Di Croco**
*7 Bay Street*
*T 9362 4678*
*www.dicroco.com.au*

**084 Cloth**
*54a Carrington Road*
*T 9326 7755*
*www.clothfabric.com*

**084 Woven Image**
*1a Glenmore Road*
*T 9326 0433*

**085 Wheels & Doll Baby**
*259 Crown Street*
*T 9361 3286*
*www.wheelsanddoll*
*baby.com*

**086 Space**
*84 O'Riordan Street*
*Sydney*
*T 8339 7588*
*10 James Street*
*Brisbane*
*T 07 3253 6000*
*Millenia Walk Level 2*
*9 Raffles Boulevard*
*Singapore*
*T 00 65 6415 0000*
*www.spacefurniture.*
*com.au*

# SPORTS AND SPAS

**088 Fitness First**
*www.fitnessfirst.com.au*

**088 Sydney Cricket Ground**
*Moore Park Road*
*T 9360 6601*
*www.sydneycricket*
*ground.com.au*

**089 Spa Chakra**
*Blue, Sydney*
*6 Cowper Wharf Road*
*T 9368 0888*
*www.spachakra.com*

**090 North Sydney Olympic Pool**
*4 Alfred Street South*
*T 9955 2309*
*www.northsydney.*
*nsw.gov.au*

**092 King George V Recreation Centre**
*Cumberland Street*
*T 9244 3600*

**094 City Gym**
*107-113 Crown Street*
*T 9360 6247*
*www.citygym.com.au*

# ESCAPES

**096 Brokenwood**
*401-427 McDonalds Road*
*Pokolbin*
*Hunter Valley*
*T 4998 7559*
*www.brokenwood.com.au*

**096 McWilliam's Mount Pleasant Estate**
*Marrowbone Road*
*Pokolbin*
*Hunter Valley*
*T 4998 7505*
*www.mcwilliams.com.au*

**096 Small Winemakers Centre**
*426 McDonalds Road*
*Pokolbin*
*Hunter Valley*
*T 4998 7668*

**096 Sydney By Seaplane**
*www.sydneybysea
plane.com*

**097 Jonah's**
*69 Byna Road*
*Palm Beach*
*T 9974 5599*
*www.jonahs.com.au*

**097 Palm Beach Water Sports**
*Governor Phillip Park*
*T 0408 862 000*

**098 Tonic**
*251 Talga Road*
*Lovedale*
*Hunter Valley*
*T 4930 9999*
*www.tonichotel.com.au*

**098 Shakey Tables**
*1476 Wine Country Drive*
*North Rothbury*
*Hunter Valley*
*T 4938 1744*
*www.shakeytables.com.au*

**100 Huski**
*Sitzmark Street*
*Falls Creek*
*Victoria*
*T 1300 652 260*
*www.huski.com.au*

**102 Echoes Boutique Hotel & Restaurant**
*3 Lillanfels Avenue*
*Katoomba*
*T 02 4782 1966*

**102 Mecure Grand Hydro Majestic**
*Great Western Highway*
*Meadow Bath*
*T 02 4788 1002*

## WALLPAPER* CITY GUIDES

**Editorial Director**
Richard Cook

**Art Director**
Loran Stosskopf
**City Editor**
Carrie Hutchinson
**Series Editor**
Jeroen Bergmans
**Project Editor**
Rachael Moloney
**Series Retail Editor**
Emma Moore
**Executive**
**Managing Editor**
Jessica Firmin

**Chief Designer**
Ben Blossom
**Designers**
Dominic Bell
Sara Martin
Ingvild Sandal
**Map Illustrator**
Russell Bell

**Photography Editor**
Emma Blau
**Photography Assistant**
Jasmine Labeau

**Sub-Editor**
Paul Sentobe
**Editorial Assistant**
Milly Nolan

**Wallpaper* Group**
**Editor-in-Chief**
Jeremy Langmead
**Creative Director**
Tony Chambers
**Publishing Director**
Fiona Dent

**Thanks to**
Paul Barnes
David McKendrick
Meirion Pritchard

## PHAIDON

**Phaidon Press Limited**
Regent's Wharf
All Saints Street
London N1 9PA

**Phaidon Press Inc**
180 Varick Street
New York, NY 10014

www.phaidon.com

First published 2006
© 2006 Phaidon Press Limited

ISBN 0 7148 4700 3

A CIP Catalogue record for this book is available from the British Library.

All prices are correct at time of going to press, but are subject to change.

Printed in China

## PHOTOGRAPHERS

**Peter Bennetts**
Huski, pp100-101

**Richard Bryant**
Rose Seidler House,
pp076-077

**Jenny Carter**
Art Gallery of New South
Wales, pp044-045

**Corbis**
Sydney City View,
inside front cover

**Ross Honeysett**
Sydney Opera House,
pp010-011
Aurora Place, p012
Eva Galambos, p071
Space Furniture,
pp086-087

Ken Middleton
Bondi Beach, p013
Sydney Harbour Bridge,
pp014-015
Ravesi's, pp028-029
Three Eggs, p041
Royal Botanic
Gardens, p042
Aria, p043
Opera Bar, p046
The Colombian Hotel, p047
Spectrum, p049
Fratelli Paradiso, p054
Cafe Sopra, p058

Billy Kwong, pp064-065
Museum of Contemporary
Art, p078
Planet, p081
Cloth, p084
Wheels & Doll Baby, p085
City Gym, pp094-095
Palm Beach, p097

**Anthony Ong**
Ruby Rabbit,
pp060-061

**Matteo Piazza**
Icebergs Dining Room
& Bar, pp062-063

**Nicole Rowntree**
Hugh Buhrich house,
pp074-075

**Jeremy Simons**
YU, pp068-069

**Andy Stevens**
Object, p079

**Adam Taylor**
Blue Mountains,
pp0102-103

**www.thomas
jacobsen.com**
North Bondi Italian Food,
pp056-057

# SYDNEY

## A COLOUR-CODED GUIDE TO THE CITY'S HOT 'HOODS

### BONDI
Babes, beach and great bars. It's not the best surf in Sydney, but it's still unmissable

### SURRY HILLS AND DARLINGHURST
Probably the best place for a temporary base, bang in the heart of boho land

### WATERLOO
Suburban, although the shops being squeezed out of Surry Hills are opening here

### KINGS CROSS AND POTTS POINTS
The sex and sleaze is more sanitised in KC these days. Potts Point is far more genteel

### PADDINGTON
Long since gentrified and now the scene of some truly spectacular shopping

### THE ROCKS AND CENTRAL BUSINESS DISTRICT
Unusually, Sydney's business district is full of beautiful parks, galleries and eateries

For a full description of each neighbourhood,
including the places you really must not miss, see the Introduction